A Day in the Life: Rainforest Animals

Jaguar

Anita Ganeri

www.raintreepublishers.co.uk
Visit our website to find out more information about Raintree books.

To order:

☎ Phone 0845 6044371
🖹 Fax +44 (0) 1865 312263
🖳 Email myorders@raintreepublishers.co.uk

Customers from outside the UK please telephone +44 1865 312262

Raintree is an imprint of Capstone Global Library Limited, a company incorporated in England and Wales having its registered office at 7 Pilgrim Street, London, EC4V 6LB – Registered company number: 6695582

Edited by Nancy Dickmann, Rebecca Rissman, and Catherine Veitch
Designed by Steve Mead
Picture research by Mica Brancic
Originated by Capstone Global Library
Printed and bound in China by South China Printing Company Ltd

ISBN 978 1 4062 1782 7 (hardback)
14 13 12 11 10
10 9 8 7 6 5 4 3 2 1

British Library Cataloguing in Publication Data
Ganeri, Anita
Jaguar. -- (A day in the life. Rainforest animals)
599.7'55-dc22
A full catalogue record for this book is available from the British Library.

Acknowledgements
We would like to thank the following for permission to reproduce photographs: Ardea **pp. 4**, **17**, **23 cub**, **23 mammal** (Nick Gordon), **13**, **23 jaws** (Thomas Marent); Corbis **pp. 6** (Flame/© DLILLC), **7**, **11**, **19** (© Frans Lanting), **12** (Encyclopedia/© W. Perry Conway), **14**, **23 prey** (Encyclopedia/© O. Alamany & E. Vicens), **20** (© Kevin Schafer), **22** (© Tom Brakefield); FLPA **p. 18** (Minden Pictures/Gerry Ellis); Getty Images **p. 10** (National Geographic/Steve Winter); Photolibrary **pp. 5** (Oxford Scientific (OSF)/Elliott Neep), **9**, **23 swamp** (Index Stock Imagery/Mark Newman), **15** (Oxford Scientific (OSF)/Carol Farneti Foster), **16** (age fotostock/Peter Lilja), **21** (Animals Animals/Lynn Stone); Shutterstock **pp. 23 rainforest** (© Szefei), **23 skull** (© Gualberto Becerra).

Cover photograph of a jaguar reproduced with permission of Shutterstock (worldswildlifewonders).

Back cover photographs of (left) a jaguar's jaws reproduced with permission of Ardea (Thomas Marent); and (right) prey reproduced with permission of Photolibrary (Oxford Scientific (OSF)/Carol Farneti Foster).

We would like to thank Michael Bright for his invaluable help in the preparation of this book.

Every effort has been made to contact copyright holders of material reproduced in this book. Any omissions will be rectified in subsequent printings if notice is given to the publisher.

All the Internet addresses (URLs) given in this book were valid at the time of going to press. However, due to the dynamic nature of the Internet, some addresses may have changed, or sites may have changed or ceased to exist since publication. While the author and publisher regret any inconvenience this may cause readers, no responsibility for any such changes can be accepted by either the author or the publisher.

Contents

Some words are in bold, **like this**. You can find them in the glossary on page 23.

What is a jaguar?

A jaguar is a **mammal**.

Many mammals have hairy bodies and feed their babies milk.

tiger

Jaguars belong to a group of mammals called big cats.

Tigers are another type of big cat.

What do jaguars look like?

Jaguars have strong bodies with short, thick tails.

They have large heads, with strong **jaws** and sharp teeth.

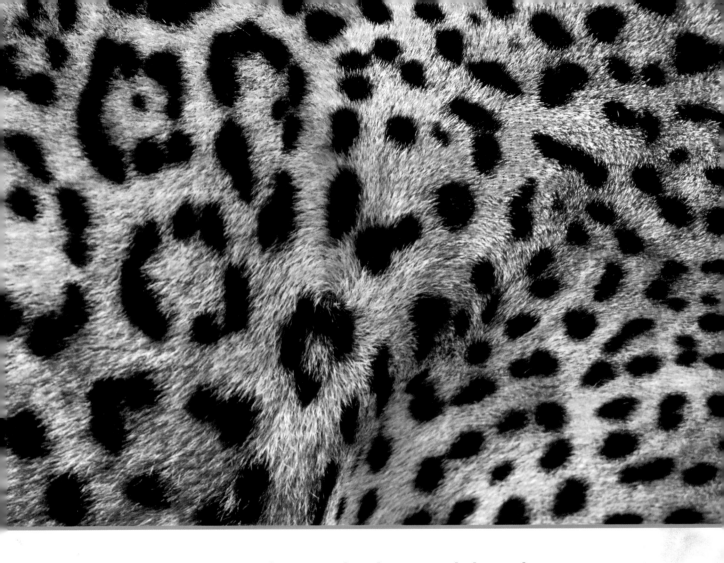

Most jaguars have light, golden-brown fur covered with black spots.

A few jaguars have very dark fur and look almost black.

Where do jaguars live?

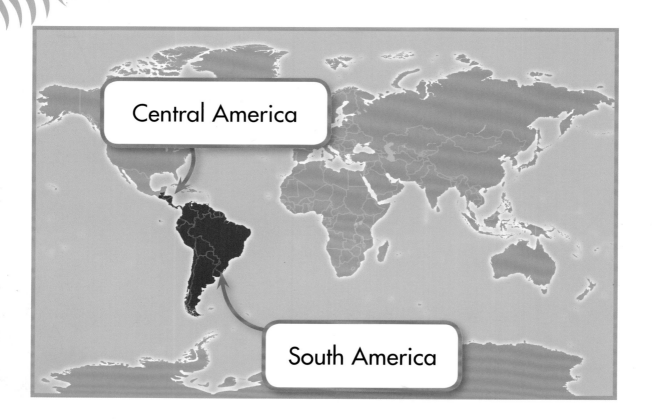

Central America

South America

Jaguars live in the **rainforests** of Central America and South America.

It is warm and wet in the rainforest all the year round.

Jaguars live near rivers and **swamps**.

They hunt for food in the water and on land.

What do jaguars do in the evening?

In the evening, jaguars start hunting.

A jaguar may carry on hunting all night.

Jaguars have special eyes that can see in dim light.

This helps the jaguars to find their **prey** at night.

How do jaguars catch their food?

At night, jaguars hunt for **prey** in the forest.

A jaguar hides among the trees and then suddenly it pounces.

jaws

The jaguar has very strong **jaws** and sharp teeth for catching its prey.

It can kill an animal by biting right through its **skull**.

What do jaguars eat?

deer

Jaguars hunt many other **rainforest** animals.

Some of these are large animals, such as deer and wild pigs.

turtle

Jaguars also catch **prey** in the water, such as fish, frogs, and turtles.

Their teeth are sharp enough to bite through a turtle's shell.

Do jaguars live in groups?

Jaguars live on their own.

Each jaguar roars loudly to keep other jaguars away from its patch of forest.

cub

Jaguars only meet up when they are ready to have **cubs**.

Jaguar cubs live with their mother for up to two years, learning how to hunt.

What do jaguars do in the morning?

In the morning, a jaguar goes out hunting.

Many **rainforest** animals are just waking up, so there is plenty of **prey** around.

Sometimes, a jaguar stops by the water's edge.

It waits for an animal to come for a drink, then it leaps on to its prey from behind.

What do jaguars do in the day?

After hunting, a jaguar spends most of the day resting or sleeping.

A jaguar sleeps for about 12 hours a day.

Sometimes jaguars rest in caves by the riverbank.

Sometimes they climb **rainforest** trees and go to sleep in the branches.

Jaguar body map

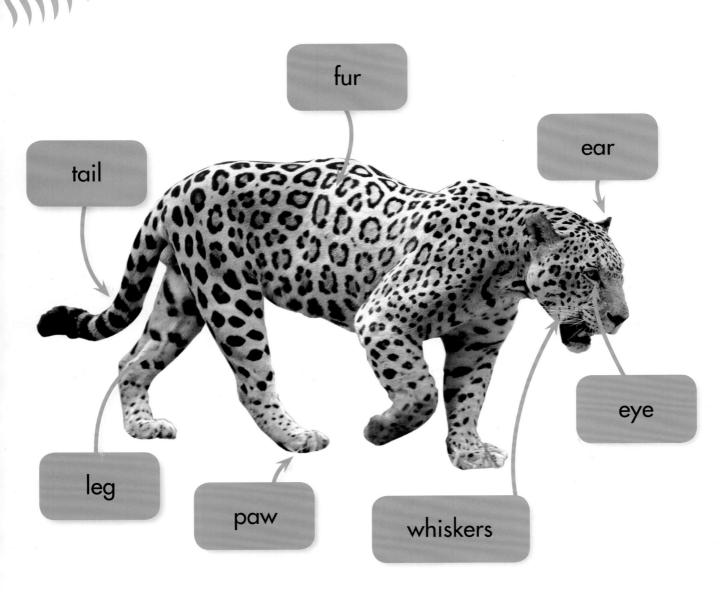

fur

ear

tail

eye

leg

paw

whiskers

Glossary

 **cub** baby jaguar

 **jaws** top and bottom parts of the mouth

 **mammal** animal that feeds its babies milk. Most mammals have hair or fur.

 **prey** animal that is hunted by other animals for food

 **rainforest** thick forest with very tall trees and a lot of rain

 **skull** bony part of the head that contains the brain

 **swamp** wet, muddy land

Find out more

Books

Rainforest Animals (Focus on Habitats), Stephen Savage (Wayland, 2006)
Usborne Beginners: Rainforest, Lucy Beckett-Bowman (Usborne, 2008)

Websites

http://kids.nationalgeographic.com/Animals/CreatureFeature/Jaguars
http://animal.discovery.com/mammals/jaguar/
http://a-z-animals.com/animals/jaguar/

Index